Daemonolatry Goetia

S. Connolly
With Introduction by
Nicholas (GoeticNick) Schneider

Daemonolatry Goetia

S. Connolly
With Introduction by
Nicholas (GoeticNick) Schneider

DB Publishing
United States of America

DB Publishing is an imprint of Darkerwood Publishing Group, PO Box 2011, Arvada, CO 80001. Contact the publisher for bulk purchases and discounts or contact ofs.admin@gmail.com for online wholesale purchase links.

ISBN: 978-0-9669788-2-7

Book Design by DB Publishing, Adrianna.
Cover Design: Adrianna

For TAJ
Despite the fact that we had our differences, you
have been missed. Since you couldn't write it, I did.
Rest in Peace

INTRODUCTION

I met S. Connolly about six years ago through mutual friends. I admit that at the time I did not expect that the quiet, thoughtful woman I'd been introduced to was actually a very competent working magician that I would later come to respect a great deal. At that time, she had delved into Goetia and was quite familiar with the original texts, but like many who work with the Goetic Daemons and Goetia by-the-book, had a biased opinion based on the Judaic background of the material.

I like to think it was partly me, and partly the Goetic Daemons, who changed her mind. I know for a fact that for the better part of five years, at my suggestion and the suggestion of other Goetic Daemonolaters, she studied Goetia extensively, discussed it with myself and other Goetic Daemonolaters at length, and worked with all 72 Goetic spirits and the four great kings repeatedly. When it was all said and done about a year ago she sent me an e-mail.

It read, *"I am a big enough person to admit it when I'm wrong. Once I stripped away the church-clothes this became amazing material. Thank you for giving me a different perspective and convincing me to give it a second go. How about you, Ellen and I write a modified Goetia specifically for Daemonolaters?"* It was at that moment the idea for this book was born.

1

Most certainly many Goetic Daemonolaters have been modifying Goetia for years. Goetic Daemonolaters have been around long before me and at least as long as our friend Ellen Purswell started working with Goetic Daemons back in the 1950's.

Originally I was going to co-author this book, but time and other obligations made that impossible. Instead, I acted as editor and consultant and I was given the privilege of being able to introduce this book.

I have to say that I am not sorry I didn't write it.

I think S. Connolly has done a wonderful job, probably in more detail and depth than I would have done. It's a short book to be sure, but so is the original Goetia.

This book has already done the modifications for you and is just another alternative viewpoint of the Goetia. I am confident that practitioners of Daemonolatry, practitioners of grimoiric magick, collectors of books about Goetia, and even students of Goetia will all find something useful in this book, even if it is just a unique viewpoint.

Many of S. Connolly's observations of the Goetic Daemons are insightful as are her thoughts on the modifications of the Goetic ritual itself. Even I, someone who has been working with Goetic Daemons for over twenty-five years, got a great deal of insight and inspiration from this book.

For the first time in the male dominated world of ceremonial and grimoiric magick, here is a Goetia coming to you from both a Daemonolatry and a female perspective. To my knowledge Ms. Connolly is the first female magician to really delve into the guts of Goetia publicly and in book form. This is the new go-to-guide for Goetic Daemonolaters.

For a companion guide, an adept's commentary about Daemonolatry and working with Goetic Daemons, be sure to pick up Ellen Purswell's book *Goetic Demonolatry.*

~Nicholas "GoeticNick" Schneider

ABOUT THIS GOETIA

Originally this book was going to be written by myself and both Ellen Purswell and Nicholas Schneider, but due to time constraints and day-to-day life obligations that is not how it worked out. Instead, both of them consulted on this work and Goetic Nick edited. So I would like to take a quick moment to thank them both for their encouragement, support, insight, and time spent reviewing the manuscript.

This work is a collection of five years of my experience and experimentation in working with the Goetic Daemons using Daemonolatry methods. I have noted the difference in how to construct your circle and alternative viewpoints of the Triangle of Art, thus converting the original Goetic system to something far more workable for those who worship (respect and hold in high regard) the Goetic Divine Intelligences (Daemons).

Hence Daemonolatry Goetia.

The book first discusses how to prepare your ritual space and preparations of the magical tools, then goes into the upper hierarchy of the Daemonic above the Goetic spirits, and finally delves into each of the 72 Goetic Spirits sharing their Sigil, Enn, Incense Fragrance, Metal, and Purpose (above and beyond what is written in existing Goetia texts).

The method of work described herein may be of great distaste to the average Goetic Magician, Thelemites, Grimoiric Magicians, and Ceremonial Magicians in general as it does not employ the use of "protective" circles or spiritual condoms of any sort. Please know up front that in using these methods I am **NOT** saying Goetic Daemons (or Daemons in general) cannot be dangerous. They most certainly can be if approached with instability, arrogance, or disdain.

Nor am I saying that the magician shouldn't be cautious. Anyone who isn't cautious to some degree is a fool. So no - I do not treat Daemons as if they're innocent fluffy rabbits or cute baby polar bears. But rather I treat them respectfully as teachers. Yes, sometimes those teachers will knock you on your ass. When that happens, you probably needed it or deserved it. Hindsight is 20/20.

Ultimately what I am saying is I believe (as it has been my experience) that if approached with respect and a genuine intent to seek out Daemonic wisdom, most Daemons are quite obliging and will treat the practitioner likewise. Expect a Daemon to mirror yourself back at you. So if you come at a Daemon with fear - they'll give you something to fear. You approach a Daemon with anger - they'll come back at you with anger. If you approach a Daemon with arrogance - you might get a not-so-nice ego slap-down.

For those persons who see Daemons as parts of our own psyche that need to be controlled and pushed around, then by all means -- practice evocation and Goetia as prescribed by the original texts or even

Thelema modifications. However, consider this: If you view the Daemon as merely part of you, shouldn't you respect yourself? Pushing oneself around, threatening the self into submission -- is that really the only way you can manifest internal change within yourself? I realize and respect that some people can only effect self-change by kicking their own ass. However, the Daemonolatry magician often sees the Daemonic as both internal and external and in learning to respect the Self and know our own faults, we can better navigate our internal oceans without having to constantly fight against our nature. As above, so below.

My opinion is certainly not gospel, just a different viewpoint.

So all this said, I respectfully submit my Daemonolatry Goetia for your use and enlightenment.

S. Connolly

PREPATORY WORK

The original Goetia came replete with very detailed instructions on how the magician should create all tools, seals, and how the circle should be set up. As you know, Daemonolatry/Demonolatry means Demon Worship. So the traditional evocation of Goetic Daemons seems a bit disrespectful to most of us. Especially since some of the Daemons are actually just old Gods. Now sure, if you're pulling the Daemonic from within yourself and you're unable to conjure the appropriate Daemonic force from within yourself, perhaps evocation has its place. However, as Daemonolaters, we are viewing the Goetic Daemons as Divine Intelligences both internal and external.

This particular section of the book will explain to you how some Daemonolaters, myself included, have modified the existing material, tools, and circle construction for the sake of creating a respectful ritual space within which to work.

ABOUT THE WORKING

The original manuscript starts out explaining the timing of the ritual. For those of you familiar with planetary spirit evocation and Heptameron ritual construction (among others), this will not be new to you. For the rest of you, the Goetia starts by explaining that moon phase is important to the work and that you should perform Goetic work when the moon is 2, 4, 6, 8, 10, 12, or 14 days old. That means the first fourteen days after the new moon on EVEN numbered days. This is probably because most magicks for new beginnings, starting new projects, and making changes are often done during the first 14 days of a moon cycle. However, the authors want the magician to note that this is not gospel. If you are invoking Focalor and Valefor to curse your enemy, you can and should not hesitate to perform the work during a dark moon if it suits you.

Next, the text discusses how the seals of the Daemons should be made in the metal of their station. *"The Chief Kings' in Sol (Gold); Marquises' in Luna (Silver); Dukes' in Venus (Copper); Prelacies' in Jupiter (Tin); Knights' in Saturn (Lead) Presidents' in Mercury (Mercury); Earls' in Venus (Copper), and Luna (Silver)"*

I have found that sigils/seals can be made on paper with appropriate colors, or in clay with appropriate colors as needed. Some magicians merely write the sigils down on parchment squares. You may be able

8

to find a supplier of disks in various metals, but you'll also need to invest in some engraving supplies if you're going to do this. Many of us Daemonolaters who do work with Goetia suspect a great deal of the elaborate instruction in the old grimoires like Goetia was merely meant to dissuade the uninitiated from trying the work. After all, working with Daemons is clearly not something one does for a Saturday night kick.

The text then goes on to discuss the Four Great Kings of Goetia (what, you only thought there were 72?) These kings are Amaymon, Corson, Zimimay (Ziminair, Zimimar etc...), and Goap. These Four Great Kings rule the four Cardinal Points as such, Amaymon; East, Corson; West, Zimimay; North, and Goap; South. Other copies of Goetia call them: *Oriens, or Uriens, Paymon or Paymonia, Ariton or Egyn, and Amaymon or Amaimon. By the Rabbins they are frequently entitled: Samael, Azazel, Azäel, and Mahazael.* This does seem to depend on the text or modification you're working from. I know I will be smote by some for saying this – but use the names that YOU most identify with.

It is suggested (in the original text) at this point the magician not call upon any of The Four Great Kings unless the situation is dire. They are also to be INVOCATED. The instructions clearly state this, even though allegedly the magician is "commanding" them to do his/her bidding. Now usually, it seems, these particular Daemonic forces are only called upon to put the 72 in line if any one of them steps out [of line].

As a note to that: A good number of Daemonolaters who specifically work with Goetia will invoke The Four Great Kings during standard Daemonolatry ritual space construction. There are also Goetic correspondences to the Nine Daemonic Divinities which you can find in Ellen Purswell's *Goetic Demonolatry*.

Then Goetia goes on to explain that The Four Great Kings can only be invoked and bound during certain hours of the day. It's been my experience that certainly you can perform your magick during the time of day conducive to the work you are doing. However, this is the real world and it doesn't matter exactly what time you perform the work. Goap will likely show at 5am just as he will at 7:22 pm. It's not like you're interrupting his sleep schedule or poker game.

All modern magicians have to make compromises to work with our schedules. All modern magicians have to make modifications based on what we can get our hands on. For those of you who believe you cannot improvise or substitute, we'll have to agree to disagree. Real working magicians improvise as needed. For those who complain that improvisation is lazy or is about doing whatever and calling it good, I actually contend that improvising and modifying existing ritual is actually more work. It seems more lazy to me to do something by the book. Substitution and modification require finding (i.e. researching) comparable substitutions and modifications conducive to the Daemon, the Magician, and the work itself.

One thing that standard Goetia does not do that Daemonolatry Goetia does do is Lucifer and Leviathan also fit into Goetia work. They are considered even higher up than The Four Great Kings.

Now back to standard Goetia. The Goetia then goes into some metal correspondences of all the Goetic spirits. I'm going to do you one better. Here is a list of all the correspondences for all the Goetic Daemons based on their "station" within the hierarchy. The station being prince, duke etc… Please note that some Daemons actually seem to fit into two "stations" (depending on the text). When this happens it is presumed you can pick and choose your correspondences.

Kings

- **Color**: Yellow.
- **Incense**: Frankincense.
- **Metal**: Gold.
- **Planet**: Sun.

Bael (Fire)
Vine (Water)
Paymon/Paimon (Water)
Balam (Earth)
Belial (Fire)
Zagan (Earth)
Asmoday (Air)
Purson (Earth)
Beleth (Earth)

Dukes

- **Color**: Green.
- **Incense**: Sandalwood.
- **Metal**: Copper.
- **Planet**: Venus.

Agares (Earth)
Barbatos (Fire)
Gusion (Water)
Zepar (Earth)
Aim (Fire)
Bune (Earth)
Astaroth (Earth)
Berith (Fire)
Focalor (Water)
Vapula (Air)
Amducious (Air)
Vepar (Water)
Uvall (Water)
Crocell (Water)
Alloces (Fire)
Murmur (Fire)
Gremory (Water)
Haures (Fire)
Dantalion (Water)
Bathin (Earth)
Sallos (Earth)
Eligos (Water)
Valfar/Valfor (Earth)

Marquis

- **Color**: Violet.
- **Incense**: Jasmine.
- **Metal**: Silver.
- **Planet**: Moon.

Gamigin (Water)
Decarabia (Air)
Cimejes (Earth)
Andrealphus (Air)
Andras (Fire)
Amon (Water)
Naberius (Fire)
Ronove (Air)
Forneus (Water)
Marchosias (Fire)
Phenex (Fire)
Sabnock (Fire)
Shax (Air)
Leraje (Fire)
Oriax (Air)

Princes

- **Color**: Blue.
- **Incense**: Cedar.
- **Metal**: Tin.
- **Planet**: Jupiter.

Vassago (Water)
Sitri (Earth)
Ipos (Water)
Stolas (Air)
Orobas (Water)
Seere (Fire)

Presidents

- **Color**: Orange.
- **Incense**: Storax.
- **Metal**: Mercury.
- **Planet**: Mercury.

Marbas (Air)
Buer (Fire)
Botis (Water)
Marax (Earth)
Glasya-Labolas (Fire)
Foras (Earth)
Gaap (Air)
Haagenti (Earth)
Caim (Air)
Ose (Air)
Amy (Fire)
Volac (Earth)
Malphas (Air)

Earls

- **Color**: Red.
- **Incense**: Dragon's Blood.
- **Metal**: Copper or silver.
- **Planet**: Mars.

Furfur (Fire)
Halphas (Air)
Raum (Air)
Bifrons (Earth)
Andromalius (Fire)

Knights

- **Color**: Black.
- **Incense**: Myrrh.
- **Metal**: Lead.
- **Planet**: Saturn.

Furcus (Air)

CIRCLE & SEAL CONSTRUCTION

Next, let's look at the circle and seal construction of your standard Goetic ritual. The original text gives very specific instructions for this. The cicle should be nine feet in diameter and on the outer edge should be written the names of the divine. This is where the Daemonolater needs to pay attention. Who is your Divine source? What names embody your perception of the Divine? For some that is the head of their hierarchy. For others, the mentor or patron/matron Daemon. Or perhaps you prefer names like Ba'al, El, Amun Ra, or Atem. Maybe even Satan for those of you a bit more direct.

So to modify the original work, use YOUR names of the divine on the outer edge of the circle.

For a visual reference of the original work see the following page.

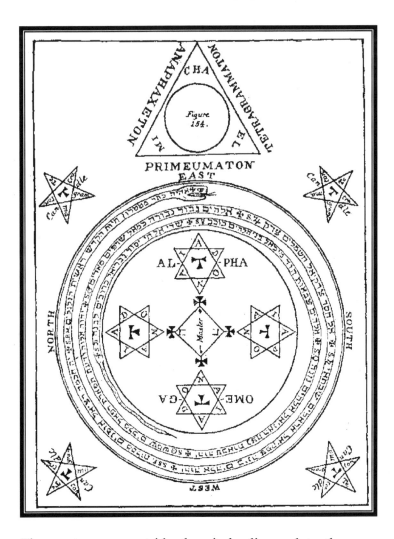

The pentagrams outside the circle diagonal to the cardinal points are sigils upon which candles are set. Instead of Tetragramaton, consider modifying the words in each triangle of the pentagram. The T in the center of the pentagrams and hexagrams are Tau. You can use the symbols for alpha and omega and consider writing Enns (while vibrating them) in the serpent coiled around the circle. Instead of

ADONAI in each of the triangles of the hexagrams, choose your own letters, words, or utterances of significance. Even sigils. Here are some modifications made by me for my own work (some of it crosses hierarchy – sorry about this – you're reading a book written by a pantheist, what did you expect?). Feel free to use these modifications, or create your own.

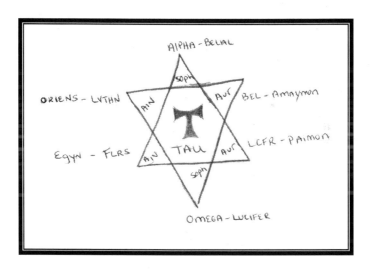

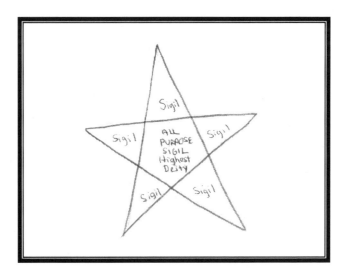

The original Goetia text also discusses, quite specifically colors that should be used for each part of the circle. Bright yellow, gold and black are all used. I suggest you create your circle in colors either conducive to the work, or choose your own colors of power. This meaning you would create the circle in the colors that "felt" most powerful to you. Some people have used wooden slats (that can be put down piece by piece to create the circle) and even painted cloth to create their circle. Others are lucky enough to have a cement floor they can paint. You can also use paper.

Now about the Triangle of Art. Traditionally the Triangle of Art is used to confine and constrain the spirit so that the magician is protected from it. Daemonolaters prefer to use the triangle as a focal point; a single point of entry in which the Daemon can come forth and communicate with the magician. What's interesting about this is in early versions of the Goetia text the circle inside the triangle is black. What else is black? A skrying mirror. Many modern Goetic Magicians have begun using the Skrying mirror in the triangle as a standard nowadays since the method was made public in several published books and demonstrative videos. A group of people in California, the OTA, began raising their triangle on an easel with the skrying mirror in place, flanked by two candles so that one person could skry while the magician/operator could conjure. A magician who can Skry doesn't need a medium in the magick circle with him/her.

Myself and other Daemonolaters actually tried this method and think it works wonderfully. Many of us endorse it. Need more information? See *The Book of Solomon's Magick* by Poke Runyon. While the authors of this book may not agree with his viewpoint necessarily – we do respect him as a magician and find his system of Goetia magick quite workable (easy to modify for your needs) and effective.

The original Goetia text explains quite clearly that the triangle is to be placed two feet from the circle (the wide end closest to the circle), the triangle must be three feet across, and most importantly *"to be placed toward that quarter whereunto the Spirit belongeth."* The point of the triangle is to be pointing toward the direction to which the spirit being evoked is situated toward. For example, if you were using a Goetia ritual construct to work with Marbas, you might situate the triangle East since Marbas is air. This part is *very* important. It means the triangle's placement is **never stagnant**. It lends credential to the practice of putting the triangle with Skrying Mirror on an easel for easy movement around the circle.

You can modify your Triangle to a more respectful "entry point" for your Daemonic visitors by changing what you write on the outer part of the triangle. Perhaps you can write Ain, Ain Soph, Ain Soph Aur, or three Daemonic names that hold some significance to you. Or, repeat the name of your Patron/Matron or Highest. You can also etch your mirror with the Daemonic Sigil of the Daemon being contacted. Of course you'd need quite a few mirrors if you plan on contacting all 72. Another alternative would be to formulate an oleum (ritual oil) for the Daemonic force being invoked and anoint the sigil of that Daemon on the reverse of the mirror. That way it can be cleaned off later.

See next page for a diagram of a modified Triangle of Art.

While making any sigil, mirror, or circle, vibrating the Enns of your highest All or the Daemonic forces you wish to invoke can imbue the work with both intent and power making for ritual with stronger results.

PREPARATION OF THE MAGICIAN

Goetia's original manuscript discusses at great length the things the magician must wear to keep the Daemonic at bay and to protect him/herself. There is a self-preparation ritual I use to help me balance myself and enter the circle with a clear intent. Firstly, there are no required vestments unless you choose to wear a sigil of your own making for balance or in devotion of the Daemons you work with. Or you can choose to wear a lamen of your Matron/Patron or Mentor. I personally prefer plain black robes or working nude.

Secondly, after some research and asking around I discovered that the ring is not something most Daemonolaters use either. You can choose to make the ring. From what I can tell, use of the ring is to keep the magician focused. Some people just have short attention spans and can get caught up in the visions a Daemonic force might give them, or get caught up in the feeling of Daemonic presence. Both can distract the magician from the intent of the ritual. The original ring contains angelic and divine names engraved on it. If you choose to make a ring, use divine names important to you. It will have more power to bring you back to the task at hand that way.

Here is my method for self-purification. Prior to the ritual the magician should bathe him or herself in clean water in which has been placed solar sea salt.

Once bathed, the magician should drink a glass of clear water blessed by Paymon or other Water Daemon to symbolize internal purification. The magician may choose to say a prayer such as, *"This water shall purge me and I shall be cleansed."*

Then the magician should dress. The original text includes prayers to be said as the magician dresses. I have modified this to, *"May these vestments be blessed in the name of [Patron / Matron / Mentor / Highest Force]."*

Then and only then may the magician perform the operation. You should also anoint yourself on the temples and third eye with a ritual oil (oleum) specific to your invocation and infused with Hyssop. For example, if invoking Vassago, use an oleum with a base of cedar mixed with calamus root or hyacinth (watery type herbs) and add some Hyssop for good measure. If you feel you need extra resolve or "protection" as it were, definitely wear the sigil of your Patron/Matron around the neck in the form of an amulet.

Some Goetic Daemonolater's also like to perform pre-working meditations wherein the magician imagines a white light coming out from his/her core being. This light extends out into the radius of the circle. This not only serves to protect the magician from imbalance (as Daemonic energy is very strong and can unbalance the unprepared magician), but can also help the magician find the inner strength to really "feel" the work being performed. That is, real arm-raising, wind in your hair type feelings from the magick.

Some people may also choose to fast for 24 hours prior to the work or to consume only a liquid diet. There are no specifications in the text for this and it is therefore optional.

The Original Magicians Ring

PREPARATION OF THE SIGILS AND THE BRASS VESSEL

Originally, the brass vessel was an important part of Goetic magick because it kept the sigils, thus the Daemonic forces, constrained inside the brass vessel. It is no coincidence that this coincides with the mythology of genii trapped inside such vessels.

Myself and other Daemonolaters prefer to view the brass vessel as a holy place to keep the permanent sigils of the Daemons you work with. It's well known that in Daemonolatry we often create paper sigils and then burn them in honor of the Daemons we work with. It is viewed that the fire alchemically transforms the love, intent, and reverence that went into the creation of the sigil from the physical to the spiritual. An alchemical transmutation and purification of sorts.

However, when working Goetic Magick, there are sigils you'll create and reuse over and over again depending on the work. While some people will create the sigils on paper that they will keep in the brass vessel, I prefer permanent clay sigils of the proper metallic color for the Deamonic force. Some magicians still may choose to do all their sigils on metal disks in the appropriate metals. Since this isn't always the least expensive method, nor the most practical, the clay works well for my purposes.

I suggest the sigils be created in a magick circle. As you are creating each sigil, vibrate the Enn of the Daemonic force it represents. Then – charge all the sigils in a pillar rite to complete the process. The sigils may need to be recharged regularly depending how often you use them. See *The Daemonolater's Guide to Daemonic Magick* for more information.

The brass vessel is another story altogether. Traditionally, as previously mentioned, the brass vessel was used to contain the sigils and thus the Daemons themselves. For our purposes, the brass vessel is merely a holy container meant to guard the sigils and keep their essence and energy in the sigil itself. Not the Daemon itself, mind you.

The container, regardless, should be large enough to fit all your sigils whether metal, paper, or clay. It should be made of brass and on it somewhere (usually the lid) should be inscribed or engraved the sigil of your All or highest Divine source. This will protect the sigils from picking up astral sludge or other energies that may sway their balance.

The Brass Vessel

PERFORMING THE WORK

In the original Goetia, once you've created all your tools, prepared yourself and your circle, you must then perform your work using numerous conjurations as you perform certain tasks. First you would light the incense fragrance with a base matching the Daemonic force you were invoking. Then there is an orison to be said when you are invoking the powers that be to protect you. Then you begin "commanding" your Daemonic force to appear with numerous threats, pulling out the sigil and threatening it with consumption by flame, forcing it to appear in the name of your highest deity. This presumably causes the Daemon to show up and enter the Triangle of Art. At this point, the magician may converse with the Daemon and tell the Demon to do his/her bidding – using the ring to protect him/herself if need be. Afterward, more threats are spoken in the name of the magician's highest deity and the ritual is closed with a banishing to make sure no Daemonic presence remains.

Clearly Daemonolatry Goetia differs greatly.

Firstly, we invoke by employing Daemonic Enns either chanted or vibrated. It is perfectly acceptable to use your own invocations as well. Since we're not trying to constrain the Daemon or force it to do anything, this alleviates the need for all the long threatening orations of original Goetic Magick. Once the Daemon is respectfully invoked, the medium can communicate with it in the mirror. Mind you that you don't just "conjure" Daemons to "get stuff". You can use Goetic method to contact the Daemonic to learn more about magickal methods, to find out if a friend has been lying to you, to bring a lover into your life, or to simply seek Daemonic wisdom. Once you've finished conversing with the Daemon, instead of issuing a strict license to depart, you would treat the Daemonic as you would a Divine Intelligence and thank it for coming, allowing it to leave in its own time. This often creates ritual spaces that dwell in Daemonic Presence. That means that eventually – you may not feel the Daemons as strongly after time because you've gotten so used to them being present. However, perform a banishing (or command them a single time) and you'll immediately feel the difference.

About now, someone in the audience screams, "But that's *so* dangerous! How irresponsible of you to tell people to do this! You're putting beginners in danger!" I guess that really depends on your personal definition of a Daemon.

I have been working with Daemons for the better part of 25 years now. Those with whom I consulted on this book have well over 65 years of working with Daemons between them and while we all admit we've had a bad experience or two with this method, it wasn't unwarranted. The Daemonic has a reason for what it does and if you need a bitch-slap, you're getting one whether you're in a protective circle or not. Period. Disagree if you will, that's fine. If these methods didn't work for us [Daemonolaters], we wouldn't be using them or sharing them with others. I've personally known other magicians who weren't Daemonolaters who were knocked flat on their backs, smacked, kicked, and bitten while working standard Goetic Magick. Interestingly enough, I have never heard of such a thing happening to a Daemonolater. Usually the smack-downs Daemonolaters get include magick going awry or something major happening in our lives right after the work. In hindsight, these events were all for the best and were often required to ensure the manifestation of the results the magician sought. Take it as you will.

From Jacob de Teramo's *Das Buch Belial*

THE FIRST CONJURATION

[Enn of Daemonic Force being invoked] I invoke and conjure you [Daemon]. I seek you in the name of [Your highest Deity]. I open this triangle unto you so that you may communicate with me. I open this triangle unto you so that you may hear my requests and help me to fulfill and manifest my will. I ask that you answer all questions with truth and clarity and grant me your wisdom without delay. If you choose to show yourself in form and shape, I ask that it be pleasing as not to invoke fear. [Enn of Daemonic Force being invoked] Come forth!

THE SECOND CONJURATION

I invoke and conjure you [Daemon] and ask that you appear and show yourself visibly to me within the triangle in a fair and comely shape without any deformity. For I seek your guidance, wisdom, and power.

THE UPPER HIERARCHY

The upper echelon of the Goetic hierarchy has been said to include Satan (the highest), Leviathan (as the Great Serpent), the Four Great Kings, and some even suggest Lilith has a place here. This is to say – there are more than 72 Daemonic forces that Daemonolaters may acknowledge if they work exclusively with the Goetic hierarchy. This may not be true for all Goetic Daemonolaters. Keep this in mind when working with Goetia as an option for additional complimentary influences or when choosing the names of your "All" when creating the framework within which you work.

There should be no need to really invoke the higher Kings in order to force the Daemonic forces to appear. However, you may choose to invoke Amaymon in conjunction with the Daemon you are invoking or to invoke the four Great Kings during a standard elemental circle construction. Some Goetic Daemonolaters believe that invoking Amaymon combined with the reassertion of the first and second conjurations make for more powerful results. I agree. Some believe you can perform the invocation of Amaymon and Satan (or your highest Daemonic force) two or three times for maximum potency. I did try this and didn't really see the need for performing each invocation more than once. Do what works best for you.

INVOCATION OF THE KINGS

Enns: Please note that there are variations of these Enns. These are the ones I use.

Depending on your preference in version of Goetia, the Kings are as follows.

King of the East - Uricus (Uriens) or Amaymon

Jen da Uriens elat
Elan Reya Amaymon
Renich Tasa Uberaca Biasa Icar [Daemonic force]

King of the South - Amaymon or Corson

Elan Reya Amaymon
Ana tasa Corson nanay
Ganic Tasa Fubin [Daemonic Force]

King of the West - Paymon or Gaap

Linan tasa jedan Paimon.
Anana avac Gaap
Jedan Tasa Hoet Naca [Daemonic Force]

King of the North - Egyn or Zimimar (also Zimimay)

Elat anan Egyn
Renin Zimimar et élan
Lirach Tasa Vefa Wehlcc [Daemonic Force]

For sigils, see Paimon. Some believe Amaymon is another name for Amon or Asmoday. Some say Gaap is Goap. There are sigils for Amaymon, Goap, Zimimar, and Corson in Carrol "Poke" Runyon's *Book of Solomon's Magick*. I really like them. They resonate with me. However, I do not have permission to reprint them here. Instead, here are some Daemonolatry specific sigils for the Four Kings courtesy of GoeticNick.

Amaymon

Corson

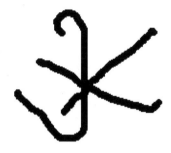

Goap

Zimimar

AMAYMON INVOCATION

Elan reya Amaymon. Oh great mighty and powerful King Amaymon who beareth rule by the power of thy supreme Satan [or highest Daemonic force] who ruleth over all the Daemonic both superior and inferior of the infernal order in the dominion of Earth, I invoke thee by your seals of creation. I seek you to answer most true and faithful my requests that I may accomplish my will and desires and to encourage [Daemonic force you are working with] to also come forth.

CONSIDERATIONS & EXPECTATIONS

There is no requirement to curse the Daemons you are invoking if they do not physically appear to you as some Daemonic forces are subtle. Also, no need to necessarily conjure the fire or burn the sigils to torment the Daemons you summon. The need for addressing the spirit with more threats is also alleviated from Daemonolatry Goetic works for that same reason. Though you may employ a formal Welcome and Depart to the Daemonic forces you summon.

What to expect when a Daemon shows itself:

First, do not expect the Daemonic to always show up in bold manifestation or bright flashes of light. You may only see shadows. You may feel a distinct change in the room climate, or you may feel an energy spike or a cold burst of air. You may hear noises or experience other paranormal phenomena, or you may suddenly feel energetic or **high**. Different Daemons feel and appear differently to each magician who invokes it. You may get full bodied physical manifestations. You should always experience a manifestation of your will (i.e. all magick performed with Goetia will manifest results if performed properly).

That is not to say Daemons are all nice and friendly. If you, the magician, require a Daemonic ass-kicking to help you manifest your will – you'll get one. Daemons are also not always tactful or gentle.

Some lessons the magician must learn are hard ones, but each lesson will make you stronger and more able to manifest your will.

WELCOME THE DAEMON

Welcome [Daemon Name] or most noble King. It was I who called upon you. (If you know your Daemonic given name, you can identify yourself by it here.)

THE RITUAL BODY

It is at this point you may make your request(s) or speak to the Daemon and ask for help, wisdom, or answers. You may also burn requests in the offering bowl at this time. You can offer a drop of your blood as well. Blood can be effectively utilized in Goetia as an additive to oleums, used to anoint the self, sigils, lamens, candles, and mirrors. To understand more about blood offerings and basic Daemonolatry practices see *The Complete Book of Demonolatry* and *The Daemonolater's Guide to Daemonic Magick*. Yes – Daemonolatry is a blood magick tradition. It should be noted, however, that blood is always taken in the least destructive way possible and usually one drop at a time via diabetic lancet device. We do not encourage self-mutilation. For women, menstrual blood is a perfectly acceptable substitution. When blood cannot be used, sexual fluids can be used in substitution. If either of those cannot be obtained, you may use saliva, skin, or hair as a last resort (in that order).

THE LICENSE TO DEPART

[Daemon Name] Thank you for diligently and willingly answering my call and questions. I bid you farewell with my gratitude. Namaah.

FINAL WORDS

This concludes the operation of Goetia. I believe that the practitioner, once (s)he understands the basics of the Goetic ritual construct and the nature of Goetic Ritual that the magician can modify and experiment from this point forward. Remember that this book is just a starting point and it's certainly not gospel.

A Note About The Sigils:

Please note that there are often variant sigils, even in Goetia. We have included Goetic variations if they apply. Also note that there are variant names of most of the Goetic Daemons as well. There are also some Daemons that have more than one elemental alignment and others that have more than one title. This seems to be because of variations from version to version (of the manuscripts). So if you discover variation, this is why.

Seal of Solomon

BANISHING AND SPACE CLEARING

Generally speaking, many Daemonolaters don't find they have an often or continuous need for banishing or clearing rituals. Instead, many of us practice "balancing". This will vary from person to person. Most schools of occult thought do teach that you should perform some sort of banishing/clearing before and/or after each work as a preventative measure. If you are someone who tends to attract a great deal of astral sludge because of your natural energy alignment (some people just attract it - even stable and balanced people), or if you have emotional or psychological problems and tend to attract a great deal of sludge due to that, regular banishing and/or space clearing is a wonderful idea.

Some Daemonolaters prefer to use a modified LBRP ritual or something similar as it "shoves" any nastiness out and clears all the space around the practitioner both in the physical and the astral. Yes, I realize that LBRP is actually a ritual used for ascension or to connect with the HGA. However, many people still use it to banish and clear. Use the ritual you are most comfortable with IF you need it. If you are a beginner, definitely use a balancing, banishing, or clearing ritual after every working until you understand your needs better. Check out the book *The Daemonolater's Guide to Modified Ritual* for a LBRP type ritual modified for Daemonolatry.

MANDATORY WARNING

Working with Daemons can be dangerous. Be prepared to take full responsibility for ANY magick you work.

Magick is very real. Daemonic energy is very real. If you are emotionally unstable or have a diagnosed psychological disorder please use a great deal of caution when working magick or performing any form of meditation or skrying. Magick + Mental Problems often = "episodes" including but not limited to falling back on an addiction (i.e. drugs, alcohol), psychotic episodes, severe depression, and possibly even suicidal feelings and thoughts. If your condition is managed with medication, be careful to balance yourself before and after each magickal working. See *The Complete Book of Demonolatry* or *The Daemonolater's Guide to Daemonic Magick* for more information about balancing.

THE DAEMONIC NAMES

The following pages will list each of the 72 Goetic Spirits, their correspondences, a complimentary span of holy days (agreed upon by most Goetic magicians), purpose (both Traditional and the Author's Notes), and their sigils.

There may be additional sigils for each Daemonic force and the Daemons may even share with you sigils for them that are specific to you. The only sigils I have included in this book are the Goetic (both circled and un-circled as I like the creativity of the raw sigils). See *The Daemonolater's Guide to Daemonic Magick* or *The Complete Book of Demonolatry* to compare sigils of Daemons that cross hierarchies. Use the sigils circled if you want to invoke the Daemon specifically or un-circled if you want to invoke the Daemon generally.

You'll notice that I, in all instances, have added additional purposes for each Daemon. I've found the Goetia descriptions quite limiting and feel they do not explore the full potential of each Daemonic spirit/force. You may find additional benefits of these Daemons beyond what's listed as you work with them.

Please know that when it comes to incense scents, the incense listed is the base scent. This means that you can add additional herbs or scents to the base perfumes if you choose to do so! You might do this if you want your incense to include attributes aside from the Damonic. For example, let's say you are performing a working to find a lover. You are working with Sitri so you'd use Cedar as your base scent, but you might choose to additionally add an herb or plant matter aligned with Venus. Or a personal scent based on your own elemental alignment or your Patron. These are merely examples to show you how you can effectively modify and make each working more personal to your Self while still honoring the preferences of the Daemonic force being invoked.

Please note you'll notice 2 Daemons for each date frame. The first pass (of the year) starting with Bael are Day Daemons. The second pass (of the year) starting with Phenex are Night Daemons.

For the original descriptions of what the Daemons allegedly look like, you can reference any copy of Goetia. I have not included physical descriptions here simply because I believe (based on personal experience) that Daemons tend to appear as the magician expects them to appear. I prefer to keep an open mind about that. To me Leviathan appears as a tall, black-haired blue-eyed man. To others, *she* appears as a beautiful woman.

Bael

KING

Color: Yellow.
Incense: Frankincense.
Metal: Gold.
Planet: Sun
Element: Fire
Enn: *Ayer Secore On Ca Bael*
Date: March 21- March 30

Original Purposes: Invisibility

Author's Notes: Some view Ba'el as the fire part of Ba'al. He rules over solstices and fire festivals and can bring together friends. He can spark creativity and instruct people in matters of the heart. If you seek him for wealth, let it be in creative wealth or wealth created by creative projects. It is suggested you wear his sigil when invoking him.

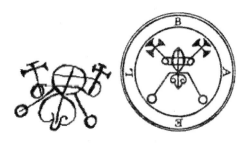

Agares

DUKE

Color: Green.
Incense: Sandalwood.
Metal: Copper.
Planet: Venus
Element: Earth
Enn: *Rean ganen ayar da Agares*
Date: March 31 – April 10

Original Purpose: Teaches languages, destroys dignities, find runaways, cause earthquakes,

Author's Notes: It is said you should wear his sigil after the work in question. Seek Agares for wisdom in friendship and to make your garden grow. He also gives advice on financial matters with regard to projects.

Vassago

PRINCE

Color: Blue.
Incense: Cedar.
Metal: Tin.
Planet: Jupiter.
Element: Water
Enn: *Keyan vefa jedan tasa Vassago*
Date: April 11 – April 20

Original Purpose: Divination (past and future), to find lost and hidden things.

Author's Notes: Contact Vassago to find out if an enemy has cursed you or is doing something behind your back. Vassago is also good counsel regarding friendship and other interactions with people. He can advise you in negotiations.

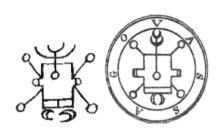

Gamigin

MARQUIS

Color: Violet
Incense: Jasmine
Metal: Silver
Planet: Moon
Element: Water
Enn: *Esta ta et tasa Gamigin*
Date: April 21 - 30

Original Purpose: Liberal Sciences and Speaking to dead sinners

Author's Notes: Also Samigina. Necromancy (to speak with any spirits of the dead). Invoke Gamigin to help in creative endeavors. An artist's Daemonic force. Seek Gamigin for inspiration.

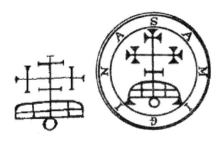

Marbas

PRESIDENT

Color: Orange
Incense: Storax
Metal: Mercury
Planet: Mercury
Element: Air
Enn: *Renich Tasa Uberaca Biasa Icar Marbas*
Date: May 1-10

Original Purpose: Uncovering secrets, causing and healing illnesses, and mechanical arts.

Author's Notes: Healing and cursing (obviously). Invoke when studying mechanics of any kind including mechanics of the human body (i.e. medicine) to retain and learn more. Invoke Marbas to cause you to see truth in any situation.

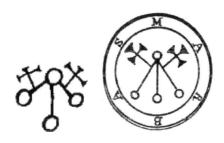

Valefor

DUKE

Color: Green
Incense: Sandalwood
Metal: Copper
Planet: Venus
Element: Earth
Enn:*Keyman vefa tasa Valefor*
Date: May 11 -20

Original Purpose: Good familiar and tempts magicians to steal.

Author's Notes: Teaches loyalty and the arts of manipulation. Can show you how to charm others and get what you want. Wear Valefor's seal during rituals to invoke, and afterward to manifest the desired results.

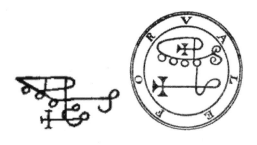

Amon

MARQUIS

Color: Violet
Incense: Jasmine
Metal: Silver
Planet: Moon
Element: Water
Enn: *Avage secore Amon ninan*
Date: May 21 - 31

Original Purpose: Predicts the future, knows the past. He can be invoked to cause or reconcile feuds between friends.

Author's Notes: Some see Amon as a fire Daemon to be worshiped at the summer solstice. Amon can help bring emotions to a head so that they can be released as usable energy. Amon can help with finding friends.

Barbatos

DUKE

Color: Green
Incense: Sandalwood
Metal: Copper
Planet: Venus
Element: Fire
Enn: *Eveta fubin Barbatos*
Date: June 1-10

Original Purpose: Can give the ability to understand animals. Finds things hidden by magicians. Knows all things (divination) and conciliates friends and people in power.

Author's Notes: Seek Barbatos to stop magician's personal wars with one another. Invoke Barbatos to communicate with your familiar if needed. Also invoke Barbatos to protect your home from hidden attacks.

Paimon

KING

Color: Yellow
Incense: Frankincense
Metal: Gold
Planet: Sun
Element: Water
Enn: *Linan tasa jedan Paimon*
Date: June 11 - 20

Original Purpose: He teaches all arts and sciences and occult. He can be invoked to bind others. To be observed toward the west and with offerings.

Author's Notes: Seek Paimon to understand alchemy. Seek Paimon for creative pursuits or to design a plan of action. Paimon can also help in emotional understanding.

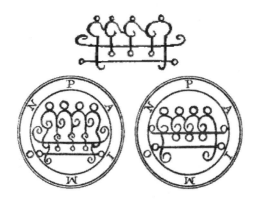

Buer

PRESIDENT

Color: Orange
Incense: Storax
Metal: Mercury
Planet: Mercury
Element: Fire
Enn: *Erato on ca Buer anon*
Date: June 21 – July 1

Original Purpose: He teaches herbalism and herbal medicines. He heals emotional discord and gives good familiars. Also teaches philosophy and logic.

Author's Notes: Seek Buer to transform the self through thought. Including rectifying addiction or bad behaviors. Invoke Buer for his wisdom about when magick is warranted and when it is not. He can help you weigh moral issues and help you distinguish between what is moral and what is natural.

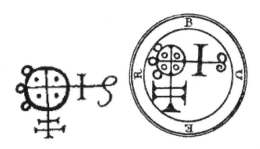

Gusion

DUKE

Color: Green
Incense: Sandalwood
Metal: Copper
Planet: Venus
Element: Water
Enn: *Secore vesa anet Gusion*
Date: July 2 -11

Original Purpose: He knows all past, present and things to come. He can answer questions and tell you why you ask them. He conciliates and reconciles friendships and gives honor and dignity to those who seek it.

Author's Notes: If you are looking to find your faults or to do deep self-work, Gusion is the Daemon to work with. He holds a mirror up to your face and causes you to see your true self.

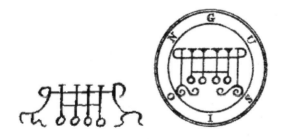

Sitri/Sytry

PRINCE

Color: Blue
Incense: Cedar
Metal: Tin
Planet: Jupiter
Element: Earth
Enn: *Lirach Alora vefa Sitri*
Date: July 12 - 21

Original Purpose: Sitri is a lust demon and causes men and women to be passionate and get naked around one another.

Author's Notes: Invoke Sitri for seduction rituals (become Incubi or Succubi). Invoke Sitri during sex magick to boost the energy raised. Sitri can also be called up when you seek to infuse any creative project with passion. I saw Sitri as feminine and Fire.

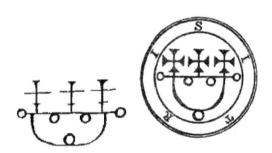

Beleth

KING

Color: Yellow
Incense: Frankincense
Metal: Gold
Planet: Sun
Element: Earth
Enn: *Lirach tasa vefa wehlc Beleth*
Date: July 22 – August 1

Original Purpose: Beleth is described as terrifying and it is said the magician must keep a hazel wand at the ready to keep Beleth's fury and flaming breath at bay. Causes love and desire.

Author's Notes: While Beleth can be invoked as a lust Daemon, his purpose is better suited to actual work where you are seeking a soul mate or long-term companion or stable relationship. He can also give counsel in matters of the heart and help bring rational thinking to highly emotional matters regarding loved ones. Seek Beleth after death of a loved one to find stability and comfort.

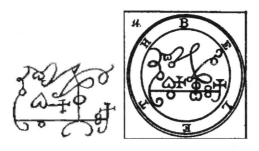

Leraje

MARQUIS

Color: Violet
Incense:Jasmine
Metal: Silver
Planet: Moon
Element: Fire
Enn: (also Leraikha)- *Caymen vefa Leraje*
Date: August 2 - 11

Original Purpose: He causes battles and strife and can cause wounds to putrify.

Author's Notes: Aside from general execration magicks, you can seek the wisdom of Leraje during conflicts in order to resolve them. Leraje also gives good counsel to those seeking help in relationships with difficult people.

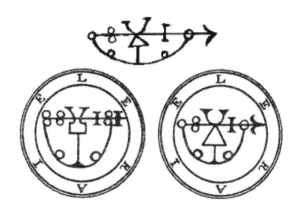

Eligos

DUKE

Color: Green
Incense: Sandalwood
Metal: Copper
Planet: Venus
Element: Water
Enn: *Jedan on ca Eligos inan*
Date: August 12 - 22

Original Purpose: Discover hidden things, knows things to come, and knows about war and how soldiers will come to meet.

Author's Notes: This Daemon is another good one to consult when seeking advice during a feud. He also gives good counsel on when to use magick and can tell you if someone is causing you harm via magick.

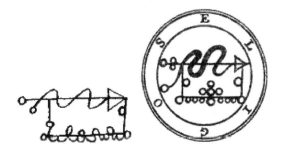

Zepar

DUKE

Color: Green
Incense: Sandalwood
Metal: Copper
Planet: Venus
Element: Earth
Enn: *Lyan Ramec catya Zepar*
Date: August 23 – September 1

Original Purpose: He causes women to love men and also makes women barren.

Author's Notes: Likewise, Zepar can be invoked as a fertility Daemon. Invoke Zepar to find your marriage partner.

Botis

PRESIDENT

Color: Orange
Incense: Storax
Metal: Mercury
Planet: Mercury
Element: Water
Enn: *Jedan hoesta noc ra Botis*
Date: September 2 - 11

Original Purpose: He tells things past and to come and can reconcile friends and foes.

Author's Notes: Most water Daemons can be invoked for emotional matters with regard to relationships. Seek Botis to draw new friends or perform divination regarding friends.

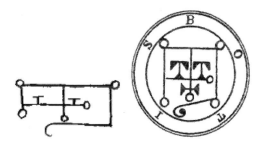

Bathin

DUKE

Color: Green
Incense: Sandalwood
Metal: Copper
Planet: Venus
Element: Earth
Enn: *Dyen Pretore on ca Bathin*
Date: September 12 - 22

Original Purpose: Knows the virtues of herbs and precious stones and can transport people from one country to another.

Author's Notes: Invoke Bathin before travel for a smooth trip. Also keep his sigil on you. You can invoke Bathin to bring you opportunity for travel as well. Kitchen witchery will get you further with Bathin than ceremony.

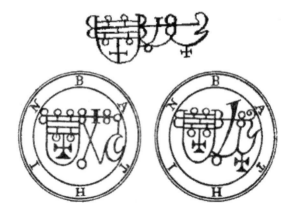

Sallos

DUKE

Color: Green
Incense: Sandalwood
Metal: Copper
Planet: Venus
Element: Earth
Enn: (also Saleos) - *Serena Alora Sallos Aken*
Date: September 23 – October 2

Original Purpose: Sallos is invoked to cause men to love women and women to love men.

Author's Notes: Comparable to Rosier in the Dukante Hierarchy. Sallos can be invoked during marriage ceremonies.

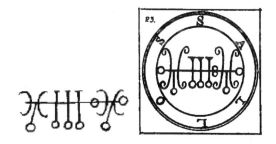

Purson

KING

Color: Yellow
Incense: Frankincense
Metal: Gold
Planet: Sun
Element: Earth
Enn: *Ana secore on ca Purson*
Date: October 3 - 12

Original Purpose: Uncover hidden things, divination, and discover treasure. Answers truthfully all questions both earthly and divine. He brings good familiars.

Author's Notes: Purson is a great Daemon to work with during Skrying or Channeling sessions when you have questions about the Divine Intelligences (i.e. Daemons) or are seeking to better understand their nature. Also a Daemon to consult before any scientific experimentation so that answers can be found. A Daemon of natural sciences.

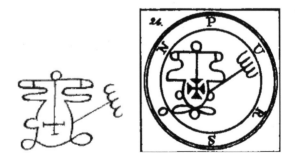

Marax

PRESIDENT

Color: Orange
Incense: Storax
Metal: Mercury
Planet: Mercury
Element: Earth
Enn: (also Narax) - *Kaymen Vefa Marax*
Date: October 12 - 22

Original Purpose: Imparts knowledge of astronomy and liberal sciences. He can also give good familiars that know the virtues of herbs and stones.

Author's Notes: Marax can come off a bit strong, like the too serious professor who doesn't tolerate the lazy student. Be disciplined when seeking his wisdom, influence, or guidance. A good Daemon to invoke before exams or during study to retain more information. His keyword is discipline.

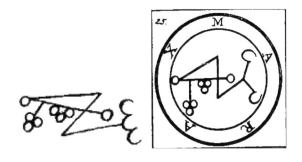

Ipos

PRINCE

Color: Blue
Incense: Cedar
Metal: Tin
Planet: Jupiter
Element: Water
Enn: *Desa an Ipos Ayer*
Date: October 23 – November 1

Original Purpose: He knows all things and makes men witty and bold.

Author's Notes: Some texts say Ipos is an Earl and can use those correspondences (Mars/Iron/Red etc…) as well. Invoke Ipos for courage or to be more decisive. Ipos can also be invoked to sort out confusion or to bring your emotions under control.

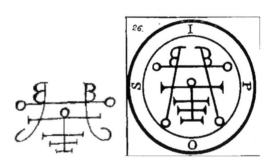

Aim

DUKE

Color: Green
Incense: Sandalwood
Metal: Copper
Planet: Venus
Element: Fire
Enn: *Ayer avage secore Aim*
Date: November 2 –12

Original Purpose: Makes one witty and gives true answers about people's private matters.

Author's Notes: The artists muse. Invoke Aim for creative inspiration or to find creative solutions to complex problems. Writers, artists and musicians should wear the sigil of Aim while working to prevent creative "blocks".

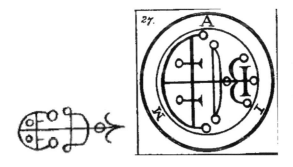

Naberius

MARQUIS

Color: Violet
Incense: Jasmine
Metal: Silver
Planet: Moon
Element: Air
Enn: *Eyan tasa volocur Naberius*
Date: November 13 - 22

Original Purpose: Makes one cunning in arts and sciences and in rhetoric. Restores lost honor and dignity.

Author's Notes: Invoke Naberius for strength and guidance to do what is honorable and right even when you fear taking a stand for what you believe in. Naberius often makes magicians feel very 'nervous'. This seems to be a natural effect of his energy. Consequently he can infuse a magician with great courage and confidence.

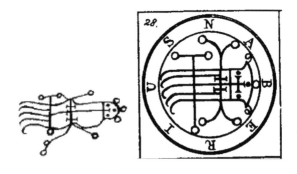

Glasya-Labolas

PRESIDENT

Color: Orange
Incense: Storax
Metal: Mercury
Planet: Mercury
Element: Fire
Enn: *Elan tepar secore on ca Glasya-Lobolas.*
Date: November 23 – December 2

Original Purpose: Teaches arts and sciences and creates wars and calamity. He teaches divination. He can make men invisible and he can cause love between friends and foes.

Author's Notes: Also an Earl in some texts. Glasya Labolas can be invoked to keep what you're doing a secret from others. To make you 'invisible' per se. He can make you wise to what is really going on around you and can make your friends and enemies unsuspecting. You could certainly work with him for execration/binding, but also to keep projects secret from nosey co-workers or competitors or to keep a surprise party from a friend.

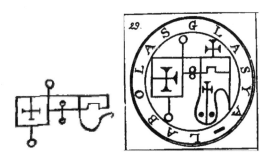

Bune

DUKE

Color: Green
Incense: Sandalwood
Metal: Copper
Planet: Venus
Element: Earth
Enn: (also Bime) – *Wehlc melan avage Bune Tasa*
Date: December 3 - 12

Original Purpose: He gives truthful answers, he can part the veil between the living and the dead and gather the dead. He can give riches and make a magician wise and well-spoken.

Author's Notes: Bune is one of the Goetia's Necromancy Daemons. If you have a medium ready to channel the dead, invoke Bune to keep order and peace during the séance. He can impart understanding and wisdom about the nature of death.

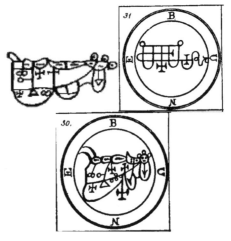

Ronove

MARQUIS

Color: Violet
Incense: Jasmine
Metal: Silver
Planet: Moon
Element: Air
Enn: *Kaymen vefa ronove*
Date: December 13 - 21

Original Purpose: Imparts the knowledge of tongues and favors of friends and foes. He also gives good servants and teaches rhetoric.

Author's Notes: The Daemon of Knowledge and Wisdom in the Dukante Hierarchy. Ronove can also be invoked to cause people to see your way of thinking or feel the need to help you. Be careful of invoking Ronove to control others because it will often turn into a lesson for your benefit.

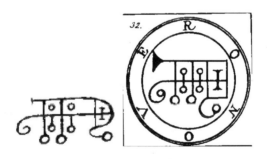

Berith

DUKE

Color: Green
Incense: Sandalwood
Metal: Copper
Planet: Venus
Element: Fire
Enn: *Hoath redar ganabal Berith*
Date: December 22 - 30

Original Purpose: Will give truthful answers. Can turn all metals to gold. He can give dignities. The original Goetia gives warning that Berith is a liar.

Author's Notes: Berith seems to prefer the magician to come to the correct answer on his own and will often impart mistruths to impart lessons. This seems to be a method of instruction rather than something done underhandedly. A Daemon of alchemy. Can teach the magician to help himself.

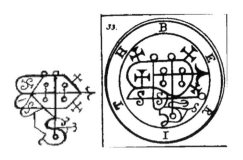

Astaroth

DUKE

Color: Green
Incense: Sandalwood
Metal: Copper
Planet: Venus
Element: Earth
Enn: *Tasa Alora Foren Astaroth*
Date: December 31 – January 9

Original Purpose: Can tell the truth and reveal all secrets. Can make men knowing of the liberal sciences and evidently knows the fall mythology (Milton's Paradise Lost) by heart.

Author's Notes: A Daemoness of Divination. Invoke her for skrying especially. She is also a Daemoness of friendship and love and can help you find these things.

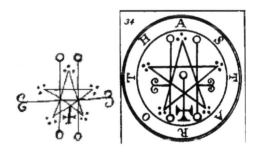

Forneus

MARQUIS

Color: Violet
Incense: Jasmine
Metal: Silver
Planet: Moon
Element: Water
Enn: *Senan okat ena Forneus ayer*
Date: January 10 - 19

Original Purpose: Teaches rhetoric and languages. Gives men a good name and can cause one's enemies and friends to love him.

Author's Notes: Invoke Forneus to influence others to favor you. Invoke Forneus before legal battles to get favorable results.

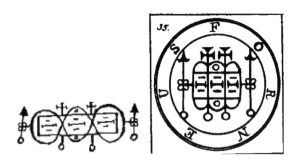

Foras

PRESIDENT

Color: Orange
Incense: Storax
Metal: Mercury
Planet: Mercury
Element: Earth
Enn: *Kaymen vefa Foras*
Date: January 20 -29

Original Purpose: Knowledge of herbs and stones. Teaches logic and ethics and helps men live long and in good health. Can give treasure and find lost items.

Author's Notes: Seek Foras to solve problems, especially those of a business nature. Foras gives stability and a clear head.

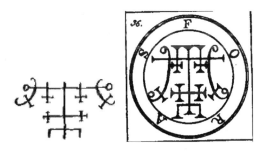

Asmoday

KING

Color: Yellow
Incense: Frankincense
Metal: Gold
Planet: Sun
Element: Air
Enn: *Ayer avage Aloren Asmoday aken*
Date: January 30 – February 8

Original Purpose: He is keeper of the ring of virtues and can give said ring. He can lead the magician to treasure, make him invincible, and will give true answers to demands. He also teaches mathematics, astronomy and crafts.

Author's Notes: Some believe Asmoday is one of three the three heads (the others being Amaymon and Amducius) in the Asmodai image in Collin DePlancy's *Dictionnaire Infernal*. Some believe Asmoday is equal to Asmodeus, a Daemon of lust and passion. Asmoday can be worked with to make the magician physically stronger and mentally sharp.

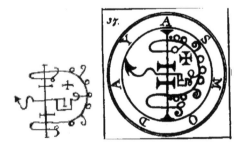

Gaap

PRESIDENT

Color: Orange
Incense: Storax
Metal: Mercury
Planet: Mercury
Element: Air
Enn: *Deyan Anay Tasa Gaap*
Date: February 9 - 18

Original Purpose: He can steal other mages familiars and give them to you. He has the power to render men ignorant or to give them great wisdom and knowledge. He can teach you to consecrate things in the name of Amaymon. He can move people from one kingdom to another. He also seems to teach philosophy, liberal science, can cause both love and hatred, and tell you anything you want to know.

Author's Notes: Also listed as a Prince. Invoke Gaap to render others' magick or power inert while enhancing your own.

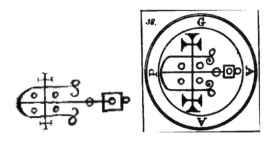

Furfur

EARL

Color: Red
Incense: Dragon's Blood
Metal: Copper or Silver
Planet: Mars
Element: Fire
Enn: *Ganen menach tasa Furfur*
Date: February 19 - 28

Original Purpose: A lord of storms, he can spark love between men and women. He can answer questions about the secret and the divine. Allegedly he won't speak the truth unless compelled.

Author's Notes: Invoke Furfur to raise energy during a ritual or before. Furfur is the Daemon of fire skrying. It's not that he won't speak the truth but rather you have to ask the right question and he will tell you whatever you want to know.

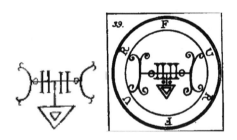

Marchosias

MARQUIS

Color: Violet
Incense: Jasmine
Metal: Silver
Planet: Moon
Element: Fire
Enn: *Es na ayer Marchosias Secore*
Date: March 1 - 10

Original Purpose: A warrior.

Author's Notes: Marchosias can teach discipline and coping skills. He can be invoked that the magician may learn to control his own temper and wield it as a warrior might his sword. Seek Marchosias for confidence, courage, and strength.

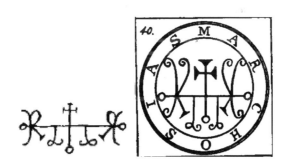

Stolas

PRINCE

Color: Blue
Incense: Cedar
Metal: Tin
Planet: Jupiter
Element: Air
Enn: (also Stolos)– *Stolos Ramec viasa on ca*
Date: March 11 -20

Original Purpose: Teaches astronomy and the properties of herbs and stones.

Author's Notes: Stolas is another "teacher" Daemon. Invoke him to learn witchcraft or sciences of the natural world (i.e. biology, geology, botany, etc..). Wear an amulet of his sigil (can be made of clay or wood as well as Tin) while learning of these things and you will retain more information and attune yourself with the natural world.

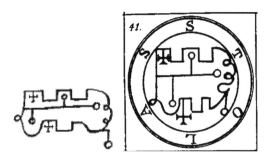

Phenex

MARQUIS

Color: Violet
Incense: Jasmine
Metal: Silver
Planet: Moon
Element: Fire
Enn: (also Pheynix, Phoenix)– *Ef enay Phenex ayer*
Date: March 21 - 30

Original Purpose: He is a poet and loves to discuss science (evidently).

Author's Notes: Another Daemonic muse for the creative. Invoke Phenex during fire baptisms and rebirth rituals including creative path working.

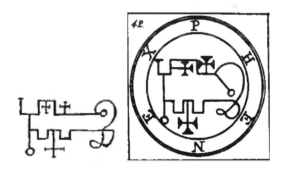

Halphas

EARL

Color: Red
Incense: Dragon's Blood
Metal: Copper
Planet: Silver
Element: Air (Fire)
Enn: *Erato Halphas on ca secore*
Date: March 31 – April 10

Original Purpose: He builds armies and fortifications, arms them, and tells them what to do

Author's Notes: Invoke Halphas to gather your allies and draw friends. Seek Halphas' wisdom in social situations where group mechanics are at play. Wear the sigil of Halphas to be well received and to command respect by those around you. Halphas is a good Daemon for Supervisors and Managers to work with to gain wisdom on how to lead.

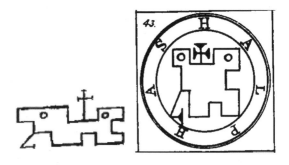

Malphas

PRESIDENT

Color: Orange
Incense: Storax
Metal: Mercury
Planet: Mercury
Element: Air
Enn: *Lirach tasa Malphas ayer*
Date: April 11 - 20

Original Purpose: He can build houses and towers and will keep you informed of your enemy's every move. He gives good familiars. Allegedly if you give him a sacrifice he will immediately deceive you.

Author's Notes: He can help you build a foundation of safety at home and in the astral temple. Some invoke Malphas as a ward against psychic and physical assaults.

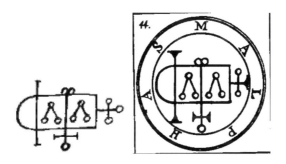

Raum

EARL

Color: Red
Incense: Dragon's Blood
Metal: Copper or Silver
Planet: Mars
Element: Air (Fire)
Enn: *Furca na alle laris Raum*
Date: April 21 - 30

Original Purpose: Steals treasure from kings. Destroys cities and dignities. Causes love between friends and foes. Tells all things past, present, and future.

Author's Notes: Invoke Raum to take down a mighty foe or adversary. Raum is also helpful in legal battles against large conglomerates. Seek Raum's wisdom to find personal strength when the odds are against you.

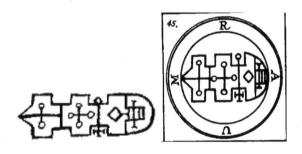

Focalor

DUKE

Color: Green
Incense: Sandalwood
Metal: Copper
Planet: Venus
Element: Water
Enn: *En Jedan on ca Focalor*
Date: May 1 - 10

Original Purpose: He will slay the magician's enemies and protect the magician if the magician commands it.

Author's Notes: Invoke for execration magicks and situations you wish to resolve quickly and in your favor. If you dream of Focalor or his sigil, it is a warning that someone wishes you ill and may be planning your downfall.

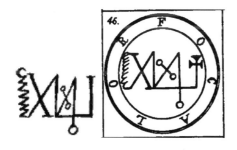

Vepar

DUKE

Color: Green
Incense: Sandalwood
Metal: Copper
Planet: Venus
Element: Water
Enn: *On ca Vepar Ag Na*
Date: May 11 -20

Original Purpose: A Daemon of water who can control ships and the waters (and storms). She can also cause men to die in three days by putrefying wounds or sores.

Author's Notes: Vepar is an excellent Daemon to invoke if you want to explore your emotions or behaviors prior to making a change. Good for cursing toxic emotions as well.

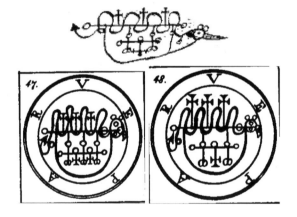

Sabnock

MARQUIS

Color: Violet
Incense: Jasmine
Metal: Silver
Planet: Moon
Element: Fire
Enn: *Tasa Sabnock on ca Lirach*
Date: May 21 - 31

Original Purpose: Builds high towers, cities, and castles and protects them. He can also make people sick with festering sores.

Author's Notes: Invoke Sabnock as a protection ward in your home or astral temple and anyone who attacks your spaces protected by him will become ill immediately. Once they call off their attack, the illness will subside. It seems to be a strong deterrent.

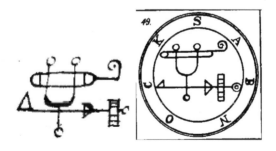

Shax

MARQUIS

Color: Violet
Incense: Jasmine
Metal: Silver
Planet: Moon
Element: Air
Enn: *Ayer Avage Shax aken*
Date: June 1 - 10

Original Purpose: Steal money from kings, fetch horses for the magician, he sometimes gives good familiars and he can take away a person's sight, hearing, and understanding.

Author's Notes: Shax is a gift giver. By gifts I don't mean material items but rather after working with him the magician might find a way to obtain something he wants. Or someone beneficial will come into his/her life. Sometimes Shax will temporarily take something from you only to give it back once you've learned to appreciate it.

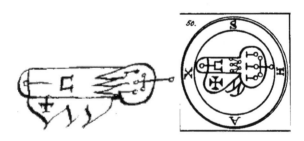

Vine

KING

Color: Yellow
Incense: Frankincense
Metal: Gold
Planet: Sun
Element: Water
Enn: *Eyesta nas Vine ca laris*
Date: June 11 -20

Original Purpose: Sometimes listed as an Earl. He can build towers, destroy walls and conjure great storms. He is also about discovering hidden things including much about magick.

Author's Notes: Vine is a magician's Daemon. Invoke him when you want to learn more about magick or you wish to better understand something you're studying (with regard to magick).

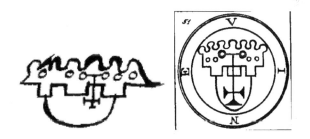

Bifrons

EARL

Color: Red
Incense: Dragon's Blood
Metal: Copper or Silver
Planet: Mars
Element: Earth
Enn: *Avage secore Bifrons remie tasa*
Date: June 21 – July 1

Original Purpose: Lights candles on the graves of the dead and can invoke the dead. He can make a man knowledgeable in astronomy and other sciences. He can teach the properties of stones and woods.

Author's Notes: Another Necromancy Daemon. Work with Bifrons to communicate with the dead. This would be the Daemon invoked for a funeral ceremony to help usher the dead on their journey. Also invoke during rituals to honor ancestors or to learn to accept death.

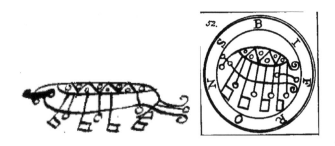

Uvall

DUKE

Color: Green
Incense: Sandalwood
Metal: Copper
Planet: Venus
Element: Water
Enn: (also Vual or Voval)– *As ana nany on ca Uvall.*
Date: July 2 -11

Original Purpose: A Daemon of friendship and love.

Author's Notes: Wearing the sigil of Uvall when going to a party or social gathering will draw people to you.

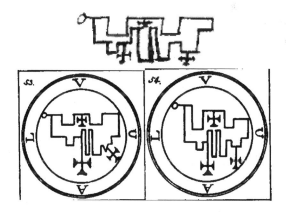

Haagenti

PRESIDENT

Color: Orange
Incense: Storax
Metal: Mercury
Planet: Mercury
Element: Earth (Water)
Enn: *Haagenti on ca Lirach*
Date: July 12 - 21

Original Purpose: Makes men wise, turns water to wine, all metals to gold etc…

Author's Notes: A Daemon of alchemical transformation. Can take something ordinary or negative and help you change it into something extraordinary. For example, if life gives you lemons, make lemonade.

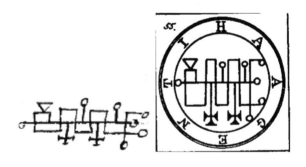

Crocell

DUKE

Color: Green
Incense: Sandalwood
Metal: Copper
Planet: Venus
Element: Water
Enn: *Jedan tasa Crocell on ca*
Date: July 22 – August 1

Original Purpose: Teaches liberal science and geometry. He can find water and warm it.

Author's Notes: Another Water Daemon. Invoke Crocell to soften aggressive or sharp emotions and warm the cold-hearted. Crocell can help people see the other side of an argument and not be so quick to judge.

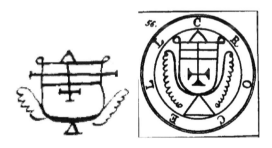

Furcus

KNIGHT

Color: Black
Incense: Myrrh
Metal: Lead
Planet: Saturn
Element: Air
Enn: *Secore on ca Furcas remie*
Date: August 2 -11

Original Purpose: Teaches pyromancy, astrology, chiromancy, logic and philosophy.

Author's Notes: Work with Furcus when learning to read natal charts, palms or learning clairvoyant skills (including all types of skrying, not just pyromancy). Note that Furcus takes his arte very seriously and expects those who seek him to do the same. If you are not serious, expect a stern "smack down".

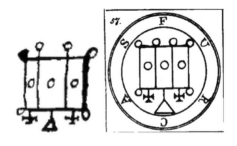

Balam

KING

Color: Yellow
Incense: Frankincense
Metal: Gold
Planet: Sun
Element: Earth
Enn: *Lirach tasa vefa wehlc Balam*
Date: August 12 - 22

Original Purpose: He makes men invisible and witty and can tell the past, present and future.

Author's Notes: Invoke Balam to get over social awkwardness or to find the inner reasons for shyness or discomfort. Leave a piece of gold in offering to Balam (and his sigil) on the altar to keep magickal works secret until they manifest the desired results.

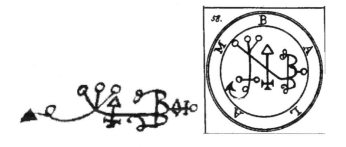

Alloces

DUKE

Color: Green
Incense: Sandalwood
Metal: Copper
Planet: Venus
Element: Fire
Enn: *Typan efna Alloces met tasa*
Date: August 23 – September 1

Original Purpose: Astronomy and drawing familiars.

Author's Notes: Invoke for helping one focus, to establish clear thinking and boundaries, and to build foundations. Some believe Alloces to be a Daemon of clay and metal artists as well as architects.

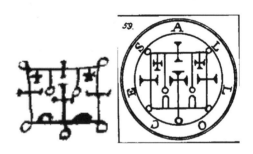

Camio

PRESIDENT

Color: Orange
Incense: Storax
Metal: Mercury
Planet: Mercury
Element: Fire
Enn: (also Caim) – *Tasa on ca Caim renich*
Date: September 2 -11

Original Purpose: He can be sought using pyromancy. He can argue your case or help you understand animals. He gives answers of things to come.

Author's Notes: I actually know a veterinarian who wore the sigil of Camio. He believed it helped him to understand the needs of his patients better. Camio can be invoked for divination of any type. Wear his sigil to *see* into any situation you encounter.

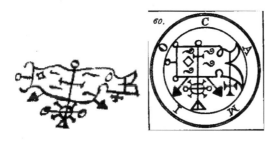

Murmur

DUKE

Color: Green
Incense: Sandalwood
Metal: Copper
Planet: Venus
Element: Water Fire
Enn: (also Murmus)- *Vefa mena Murmur ayer*
Date: September 12 - 22

Original Purpose: (Also an Earl) Teaches philosophy and can be invoked for necromancy.

Author's Notes: Murmur can keep the dead from harming the living or overstaying its welcome in possessing a medium during channeling sessions. Murmur, for me, was one of the more aggressive and intimidating necromantic Daemons of the Goetia.

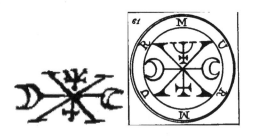

Orobas

PRINCE

Color: Blue
Incense: Cedar
Metal: Tin
Planet: Jupiter
Element: Water
Enn: *Jedan tasa hoet naca Orobas*
Date: September 23 – October 2

Original Purpose: Divination, gives dignities and favors of both friends and enemies. He also tell you the nature of the divine and the universe. The Goetia tells us he is very faithful to the magician who invokes him.

Author's Notes: Excellent to invoke for bindings and changing people's opinions. Orobas is a Daemon of wisdom. His energy is very calming. He reminded me of a tamer version of Leviathan.

Gremory

DUKE

Color: Green
Incense: Sandalwood
Metal: Copper
Planet: Venus
Element: Water
Enn: (also Gemory or Gamori) – *An tasa shi Gremory on ca*
Date: October 3 - 12

Original Purpose: She can be invoked for divination, to find hidden treasures, and to invoke the love of women.

Author's Notes: To learn Magick. Some say Gremory is akin to Delepitorae or Seshat, only less intense. I invoked Gremory to find a lost item and strangely it appeared in a place I had searched thoroughly three times.

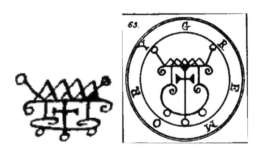

Ose

PRESIDENT

Color: Orange
Incense: Storax
Metal: Mercury
Planet: Mercury
Element: Air
Enn: (also Voso or Oso) – *Ayer serpente Ose*
Date: October 12 - 22

Original Purpose: Can change a man into any form. Can give answers about things hidden and divine (i.e. occult).

Author's Notes: To learn foreign languages or to pick up on computer or workplace skills. Also work with Ose when working magick for other people. It will help open them up to the changes (especially changes in thought or opinion).

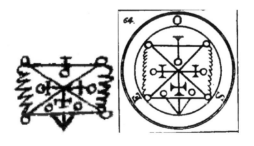

Amy

PRESIDENT

Color: Orange
Incense: Storax
Metal: Mercury
Planet: Mercury
Element: Fire
Enn: (also Avnas) – *Tu Fubin Amy secore*
Date: October 23 – November 1

Original Purpose: Can teach you liberal sciences and astrology. Gives good familiars and can give treasure kept by spirits.

Author's Notes: The spark of divinatory fire. Amy is a seer's Daemon. If you are seeking to learn about making magickal amulets, or need sigils or enns and have had difficulty getting information from other Daemons, work with Amy and your chances to get these things will increase.

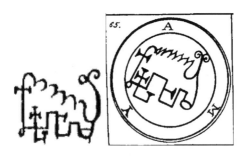

Orias

MARQUIS

Color: Violet
Incense: Jasmine
Metal: Silver
Planet: Moon
Element: Air
Enn: (also Oriax) – *Lirach mena Orias Anay na*
Date: November 2 - 12

Original Purpose: Teaches astronomy, astrology, and transforms men. He can also give you favor with friends or enemies.

Author's Notes: To make transformations to the self (i.e. the physical body). Orias can help you get physically fit and healthy. I kind of view him as a personal trainer for the willpower.

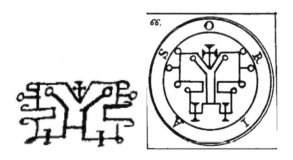

Vapula

DUKE

Color: Green
Incense: Sandalwood
Metal: Copper
Planet: Venus
Element: Air
Enn: (also Naphula) – *Renich secore Vapula typan*
Date: November 13 - 22

Original Purpose: Can make one knowledgeable in crafts and sciences.

Author's Notes: Invoke for creative business endeavors or when seeking creative inspiration. I found Vapula a bit stand-offish and untrusting. It took me five workings for Vapula to finally come forth and show me her true nature.

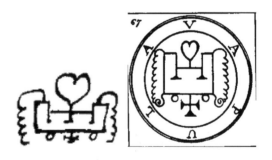

Zagan

KING

Color: Yellow
Incense: Frankincense
Metal: Gold
Planet: Sun
Element: Earth
Enn: (also Zagam) *Anay on ca secore Zagan tasa*
Date: November 23 – December 2

Original Purpose: Daemon of transmutation and transformation. Can change anything into something else.

Author's Notes: Turns things into their opposites. Invoke to help curb addictions and bad habits or to make delusional people (or dabblers) see the truth. Zagam rites are a Demonolatry Keeper ritual.

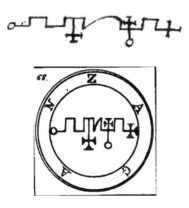

Volac

PRESIDENT

Color: Orange
Incense: Storax
Metal: Mercury
Planet: Mercury
Element: Earth
Enn: (also Valak, Valac, or Valu)– *Avage Secore on ca Volac*
Date: December 3 - 12

Original Purpose: Gives answers of where to find hidden treasures and can tell the magician where serpents are.

Author's Notes: Volac is the ultimate path-working Daemon of the Goetic hierarchy. Invoke him when you feel stuck in your spiritual growth or at a stalemate with your studies. Volac will point you in the right direction so you can find the wisdom and knowledge you seek.

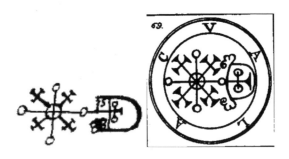

Andras

MARQUIS

Color: Violet
Incense: Jasmine
Metal: Silver
Planet: Moon
Element: Air Fire
Enn: *Entey ama Andras anay*
Date: December 13 - 21

Original Purpose: His purpose is to cause calamity of all types.

Author's Notes: To help conceal the truth from others. Invoke Andras to resolve ongoing situations between people (usually by bringing them to a confrontation). While confrontation may not be desired, it will prove a quick resolution. You may invoke Andras with any Daemon of strength or influence to give you an edge.

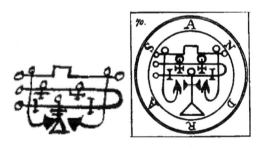

Haures

DUKE

Color: Green
Incense: Sandalwood
Metal: Copper
Planet: Venus
Element: Fire
Enn: (also Flauros, Haurus, or Havres) – *Ganic tasa fubin Flauros.*
Date: December 22 – 30

Original Purpose: He can destroy your enemies. He can tell you all things past, present, and future. He can tell you about divinity and the nature of the universe. The Goetia warns that he is deceptive and unless forced into the triangle he will lie.

Author's Notes: Also Flaros, associated with The Dukante Hierarchy Flereous and twinned with Phenex/Phoenix (different aspects of similar energy). Fire baptisms. Starting a new phase in life or new projects or relationships.

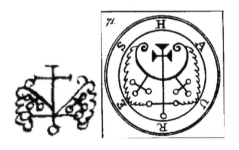

Andrealphus

MARQUIS

Color: Violet
Incense: Jasmine
Metal: Silver
Planet: Moon
Element: Air
Enn: *Mena Andrealphus tasa ramec ayer*
Date: December 31 – January 9

Original Purpose: He can transform men into birds and teach astronomy and geometry.

Author's Notes: Andrealphus can be invoked to help dissolve magick or bring a situation to a close. If you want to seal something (a spell, a portal, or a situation), Andrealphus is also your Daemon for that.

 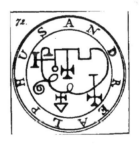

Cimejes

MARQUIS

Color: Violet
Incense: Jasmine
Metal: Silver
Planet: Moon
Element: Earth
Enn: (also Cimeies or Kimaris) – *Ayer avage secore Cimejes*
Date: January 10 -19

Original Purpose: Invoke to find lost or hidden things or to learn grammar, rhetoric, or logic.

Author's Notes: I have worked with Cimejes successfully for writing success. I've also found this is the Daemon to work with to get help with communication or to open up communication with someone. Cimejes can help job seekers network.

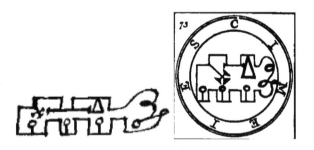

Amducius

DUKE

Color: Green
Incense: Sandalwood
Metal: Copper
Planet: Venus
Element: Air
Enn: (also Amdukias)– *Denyen valocur avage secore Amdusias*
Date: January 20 - 29

Original Purpose: Gives excellent familiars and causes trees to bend to the magician's will.

Author's Notes: Invoke during more aggressive pursuits and execration magicks. Some Daemonolaters believe Amducius, Asmodeus /Asmoday, and Amaymon are the three heads of the three headed Asmodai image from Collin de Plancy's *Dictionnaire Infernal*. Amducius being the more aggressive of the three to be employed during battle and situations requiring an aggressive strategy with military precision.

Belial

KING

Color: Yellow
Incense: Frankincense
Metal: Gold
Planet: Sun
Element: Fire (Earth)
Enn: *Lirach Tasa Vefa Wehlc Belial*
Date: January 30 – February 8

Original Purpose: Distributes titles and can make friends and enemies favor your position. He gives familiars. The magician must give offerings, sacrifices, and gifts if he wants Belial to be truthful.

Author's Notes: In the Dukante hierarchy, Belial is seen as the representative Daemonic force of earth. In this aspect, he is the destructive earth force. This makes invoking this aspect apt for execrations and necromancy not to mention business endeavors that require aggressive measures.

.

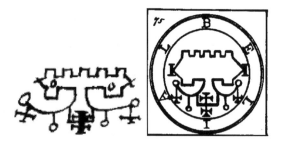

Decarabia

MARQUIS

Color: Violet
Incense: Jasmine
Metal: Silver
Planet: Moon
Element: Air
Enn: *Hoesta noc ra Decarabia secore*
Date: February 9 - 18

Original Purpose: Helps the magician discover the virtues of birds and stones.

Author's Notes: To uncover or help hide deceptions. Also seek Decarabia to free oneself of obstacles or situations holding you back. Decarabia can help the magician rise above the petty and the ego even if only for a short time.

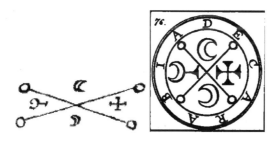

Seere

PRINCE

Color: Blue
Incense: Cedar
Metal: Tin
Planet: Jupiter
Element: Air (Fire)
Enn: (also Sear or Seir)- *Jeden et Renich Seere tu tasa*
Date: February 19 - 28

Original Purpose: Will bring certain situations to pass and to help you modify your life. He can help find thieves and lead you to treasure. The Goetia says he's good-natured.

Author's Notes: To have a clear perception of any situation or person unfettered by emotional upset or preconceived notions. I also found Seere to be good natured.

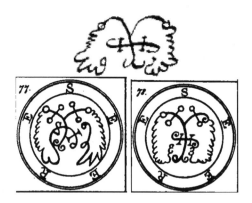

Dantalion

DUKE

Color: Green
Incense: Sandalwood
Metal: Copper
Planet: Venus
Element: Water
Enn: *Avage ayer Dantalion on ca*
Date: March 1 –10

Original Purpose: Teaches all arts and sciences and has the ability to show you the thoughts of others and to sway the thoughts of others. She can also cause love.

Author's Notes: Helps one relate with others on an emotional level. Teaches emotional intelligence and heightens empathy for others.

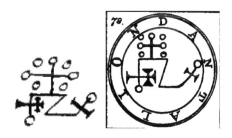

Andromalius

EARL

Color: Red
Incense: Dragon's Blood
Metal: Copper or Silver
Planet: Mars
Element: Fire
Enn: *Tasa fubin Andromalius on ca*
Date: March 11 -20

Original Purpose: To find thieves and stolen goods, invoke Andromalius. He can also help uncover plots against the magician and to punish those involved. He discovers hidden treasures.

Author's Notes: Andromalius works well for execration and protection. Invoke him as a ward in your home to protect against theft or harm against you by other people. Wear his lamen when going out alone or going to dangerous places.

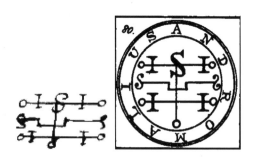

ADDITIONAL DAEMONOLATRY RESOURCES

To learn more about Goetia from a Daemonolater's perspective, see Ellen Purswell's book *Goetic Demonolatry*.

To learn more about Daemonolatry as a system of spirituality check out the book *The Complete Book of Demonolatry* by S. Connolly

To learn more about Daemonic magick from a Daemonolatry perspective see *The Daemonolater's Guide to Daemonic Magick* with S. Connolly and additional contributors.

All of these books and more can be found online at **Amazon.com** or:

http://www.demonolatry.org/

or

http://www.lulu.com/demonolatry

Printed in Great Britain
by Amazon